Extravagant Love

Stories of Hope and Inspiration During Difficult Times

Heather L. Smith

WESTBOW®
PRESS
A DIVISION OF THOMAS NELSON
& ZONDERVAN

Scripture quotations taken from The Holy Bible, New International Version® NIV®
Copyright © 1973, 1978, 1984, 2011 by Biblica, Inc. ™
Used by permission. All rights worldwide.

WestBow Press books may be ordered through booksellers or by contacting:

WestBow Press
A Division of Thomas Nelson & Zondervan
1663 Liberty Drive
Bloomington, IN 47403
www.westbowpress.com
1 (866) 928-1240

ISBN: 978-1-4908-2463-5 (sc)
ISBN: 978-1-4908-2464-2 (e)

Library of Congress Control Number: 2014901842

Printed in the United States of America.

WestBow Press rev. date: 04/16/2014

In loving memory of my brother,

Howard,

who brought me closer to Christ.

CONTENTS

PREFACE

You are deeply loved by God. You are very dear to Him. He absolutely adores you. You are His most precious creation. You are His beautiful child. You are His Beloved!

He delights in you, my friend. You are always on His mind. Nothing you can do will take away His incredible love for you. When you are lonely and discouraged, He is right there beside you, waiting to comfort and hold you in His strong arms of love.

He, the Giver of life, is perfect love. He is always patient and kind and always believes in you. He, my dear friend, is very gentle, full of compassion, and eager to encourage and strengthen your heart.

He never disappoints, criticizes, or tears down. When loved ones let you down, He is there to build you up. When the future looks bleak, He will light the way. During this difficult time, the Father is watching tenderly over you to make sure that you are all right. Cast all your anxiety on him because he cares for you (1 Peter 5:7). I am praying for you every night, my friend. The

Father has a wonderful plan for your life—to give you hope and a future (Jeremiah 29:11).

Keep trusting in Jesus. He will provide for your every need.

God loves you!

Heather

CHAPTER 1

—ɯ—

PRAISE HIM

Enter his gates with thanksgiving and his courts with
praise; give thanks to him and praise his name. For
the LORD is good and his love endures forever; his
faithfulness continues through all generations.
—Psalm 100:4–5

Dearly Beloved:

Today is the Lord's Day! Rejoice and be glad for this gift of wonderful occasions to celebrate His love for you. Look for Him, for He is not far from us. Keep your eyes focused on Christ, and you will see extraordinary expressions of His precious love for you alone. Listen to His heartbeat as He draws you close to Him. Can you feel His tender love as He cradles you in His strong arms of love? Rest in Him, for He has your every care in His control. Trust in Him, for He knows your future. It is a future of hope, for you belong to the King. He has wonderful plans for you, my friend, that will fill your heart with incredible joy. Rejoice, for our King is on His throne.

Even though you may be facing the darkest night, He will be with you through the mighty storm. He will cover you with love and whisper words of comfort and hope into your heart. He has not forgotten you, dearly beloved, because you are His precious child, and He has a wonderful design for your life. God's plan will fulfill His destiny for you and touch others with His extraordinary love.

Do not despair, for your Creator is on the throne, and He will rescue you from the mighty forces of wind and rain. So rest today, my friend, knowing that your Daddy knows where you are and will shower you with blessings from heaven while you wait on Him.

God loves you!
Heather

CHAPTER 2

—✺—

SEASONS

There is a time for everything, and a season for every
activity under the heavens: a time to be born and a
time to die, a time to plant and a time to uproot, a time
to kill and a time to heal, a time to tear down and a
time to build, a time to weep and a time to laugh, a
time to mourn and a time to dance, a time to scatter
stones and a time to gather them, a time to embrace
and a time to refrain from embracing, a time to search
and a time to give up, a time to keep and a time to
throw away, a time to tear and a time to mend, a time
to be silent and a time to speak, a time to love and a
time to hate, a time for war and a time for peace.
—Ecclesiastes 3:1–8

Dearly Beloved:

I love the seasons. I live in Virginia and am blessed
to be able to enjoy each wonderful time of the year. To me,
the whole earth is celebrating the majesty and glory of the

King of kings and Lord of lords in breathtaking splendor and magnificent beauty.

Spring is the time of birth and renewal, when tulips and daffodils lazily push their way through the warm, damp soil toward the bright sunlight smiling down at them. Forsythia and japonica burst forth in exquisite colors of yellow and red. Squirrels play hide-and-seek behind budding leaves. Robins, bluebirds, and cardinals sing songs of joy in the celebration of life.

Summer is even more beautiful. Flowers in bright profusion and rich fragrance cover the countryside and joyously proclaim the beauty of our Lord Jesus Christ. Giant oaks and pines gently wave their branches of love to the Giver of life. The mighty roar of the Atlantic Ocean proclaims His majesty and power.

Fall is my favorite season. When I lost my home and moved to a little house in the woods, fall was just around the corner. As the green leaves from a thousand trees began to change into brilliant gold, I felt like I had walked through the gates of heaven. When I came home from work each day, the sun setting in the sky had transformed the forest into a glorious panorama of exquisite beauty as piles and piles of colorful leaves welcomed me home.

And the last season, winter, is a time of quiet beauty. During this time, the earth is laid bare. Trees have lost their leaves, and the branches look like long, bony fingers. It appears that life has left the world. But wait! God will soon send snow and ice, and the barren branches are suddenly transformed into wands of light as the winter sun brilliantly illuminates the white-covered limbs. Winter is a time of solitude and reflection on the faithfulness and love of the Father. It is a time when we slow down and spend time with our families, perhaps in front of a warm fire on a cold, snowy night. It is a time when we buy gifts for friends and enjoy the bustle of holiday shopping. It is a time when we reflect on the past, enjoy the present, and hope for the future.

Our lives are like the seasons. When a baby is born, his parents experience hope and promise for the future. As the baby grows, his energy and enthusiasm bring joy and laughter. There is wonder in seeing a little one grow into a young child. As the child becomes able to do things on his own, the parents realize that he will always need them. But if they have taught him the important values of life, one day they will be able to let him go.

As the child becomes a man, he will take his place in the world. His time has come to be all God intended him to be—to use his gifts and talents. He is special and dearly loved by God. And his unique abilities will bring hope and love to others. For a season, his life will be full of decisions and responsibilities, and opportunities to encourage and inspire others who cross his path.

One day, in the winter of his life, he will lay his burdens down and enjoy the fruits of his labor. But even in the winter, a person can bless and be a blessing to the lives of the people he touches. Just as the dusk of the day is breathtaking beautiful—as the sun sets in a myriad of purples and oranges—so winter can be the most wonderful season of all.

My dear friend let me encourage you to enjoy each season of your life. As the psalmist said, "Surely your goodness and love will follow me all the days of my life, and I will dwell in the house of the LORD forever" (Psalm 23:6).

God loves you!
Heather

CHAPTER 3

—∽∞∽—

SWEET SURPRISES

Let him lead me to the banquet hall, and
let his banner over me be love.
—Song of Songs 2:4

Dearly Beloved:

God is so wonderful! It amazes me how much He loves us and enjoys surprising us with sweet gifts of love. Take Christmas, for example. The birth of our dear Savior is incredible! What a joyous occasion to celebrate the most precious gift of all, our beloved Jesus Christ. We experience days of flurry and excitement as we rush to get ready for the birthday of our King. There are presents to buy, cards to mail, loved ones and friends to call—some we haven't talked to in years. Suddenly, it is important to talk to them and convey messages of love and encouragement.

It is during this time of wonder and awe that I look for a special gift of love from the Creator of the universe—a gift especially tailored for me. I have been anticipating these sweet surprises for several years, my friend, and I have never been disappointed.

One day after Christmas, as I was driving home after spending the holidays with my daughter, I said to God, "Oh, Lord, if you really loved me, you would have one more gift for me." What a selfish request! The presents I had received from family and friends were dear, and I loved every one of them. The Father didn't seem to mind, however. When I drove into my driveway that night and walked up the steps to my little home, there was a package waiting for me. An unexpected gift of warms socks was carefully wrapped up in festive wrapping paper! The gift was simply signed, "Ann."

I was amazed. I wasn't even sure who Ann was; I knew at least two. It took several calls before I located the giver. It was the first time I had ever received a gift from her!

Last year was the best surprise of all. On Christmas Eve, I was driving up to my daughter's house. It was a beautiful drive through the countryside. Large farms dotted the landscape, and the fields were empty as farmers were resting from their work and enjoying a few special moments with their families. When I was almost there, I said to God, "Well, Lord, I don't guess you will give me a Christmas gift this year!" I really believed that. He had been faithful over prior years, but I felt that He had run out of surprises.

Dearly beloved, let me assure you that our Daddy always knows what delights our hearts. He knew the perfect gift to give His little girl. When I knocked on the door, my granddaughter answered. She was very excited but didn't share what was on her mind. I walked into the foyer and around the corner into the den. It was brightly decorated for Christmas. The tree was lit, presents were everywhere, and the pellet stove was cheerfully warming the room. Everyone was already seated at the table and enjoying Christmas dinner—everyone but one. There in the large recliner was a pretty little lady sitting and waiting for me— my dear, precious mother-in-law! She was eighty-five years old. It had been ten years since I had celebrated the holidays with her. Tears of joy fell as I hugged her. What a wonderful gift—the best present of all. I spent Christmas Eve with this sweet little lady whom I had missed so much! Later, I told God I was sorry I had doubted Him and thanked the Father for the best Christmas of all.

Dearly beloved, the Lord loves you so much. Ask Him to show His extraordinary love for you.

God loves you!
Heather

CHAPTER 4

—ᴍ—

THE JOURNEY

In all your ways submit to him, and he
will make your paths straight.
—Proverbs 3:6.

Dearly Beloved:

The night was bitterly cold as I sped down the interstate on the way to an evening class. I was a graduate student, and the spring semester had just begun. The lecture was being held at the Virginia State Capitol in Richmond, Virginia. I arrived early and walked down the deserted hall of the General Assembly building.

Suddenly, an explosion went off in my right eye! I recoiled in fear. The pain was excruciating, like someone had taken his fist and hit me squarely in the eye. I found a chair and warily sat down, trying to regain my composure. I looked around the empty building. Praise God, I could still see. The pain subsided, and I decided to stay for class.

Over the next few weeks, the pain came out and went. It was mostly bad at night. When I woke up, my eyelid stuck to the injured eye. Finally, I made an appointment with my ophthalmologist.

"A scratch has developed in the cornea of your eye," the doctor said as he handed me some ointment. "Use this at night for a month." He added, "You may have to use it for the rest of your life."

Deeply discouraged, I drove home. I didn't know what to do. Quitting school was not an option. A year earlier, I had sold my home and left a good-paying job in order to continue my education. I was almost halfway through the program, working part-time as a bookkeeper.

I continued to work and go to school. There was little relief from the pain. Eventually, my left eye grew weak from the strain. Driving to class became an ordeal. The headlights from other cars almost blinded me. Sitting in class with bright lights overhead was agonizing. For weeks, I was forced to leave before the lecture was over.

I clung to God in desperation. Every night while lying in bed, I recited Psalm 23. The words comforted me. Even though I walk through the darkest valley, I will fear no evil, for you are with me (Psalm 23:4).

In my suffering, I saw God's kindness. Many people prayed for me. Friends, family, and my church lifted me up daily. People I didn't know offered me words of encouragement. My professors were kind and gave me extensions on my papers.

I counted the hours until the semester was over. I will never forget the final night of class. A thunderstorm had developed over the city, and traffic was bumper-to-bumper on the interstate. I was twenty minutes late. The students were presenting their research papers to the class. I hadn't even started mine.

The rain stopped as I parked the car. I walked slowly to the classroom. There was no hurry now. Then suddenly, a thought came to me. *Maybe there's a rainbow somewhere.* I turned around and stared in awe. A magnificent double rainbow with brilliant hues of pink, green, and yellow surrounded the campus! In the center of the arcs, the cross graced the dome of an old Catholic church. I stayed for several minutes, reluctant to leave the majestic sight. It was like God was saying, "You made it, Heather!"

A few weeks later, I returned to the ophthalmologist for a checkup. My final paper was finished. I was anxious as I entered his office. The doctor examined my eyes thoroughly. "They look great!" he said. "Your right eye may always be weak, however," he added.

That was all right with me. When I am weak, *He is strong (See Second Corinthians 12:10).* I left the office, rejoicing and praising the Lord for His faithfulness.

My final grade for the class was an *A!* Isn't God wonderful?

Dearly beloved, the Lord loves you, too! He is your Shepherd and will watch over you always. Be anxious for nothing because He is with you.

God loves you!
Heather

CHAPTER 5

—ɯ—

MY EYES HAVE SEEN HIM

So do not fear, for I am with you; do not be dismayed,
for I am your God. I will strengthen you and help
you; I will uphold you with my righteous right hand.
—Isaiah 41:10

Dearly Beloved:

How are you today? Are you happy and celebrating life, rejoicing in God's wonderful blessings, or are you experiencing overwhelming sadness and going through a difficult time? If it is the latter, my dear, may I share some words of comfort? God sees your pain. The precious One knows where you are, my beloved. He loves you very much. You are His beloved child. The Father is your precious Daddy. He will take care of you. Lean on Him, and rest in His strong arms of love. Listen to His heartbeat and sweet whispers of love.

This past summer, I lost my youngest brother. He was only forty-four. He died tragically and unexpectedly. The pain was overwhelming as my family fought to make sense out of his untimely death. It was so devastating that I wasn't sure any of us would make it. The service was quick—just a graveside goodbye with some Scriptures read. The sorrow was so unbearable that it was hard to talk about. I found myself avoiding any mention of him to friends and loved ones.

"Oh, God," I cried, "help us." And God did. He sent signs of His love—unique expressions of love that were directly for me. I saw bright red cardinals everywhere, beautiful fireflies in the darkest night and exquisite rainbows after frequent storms. I received an unexpected note, calls of comfort from loved ones, and sweet times with Him alone as He wrapped his arms around His broken daughter.

"I love you, Heather," He whispered in the darkness. "I will never leave you nor forsake you" (*See Deuteronomy 31:6*). "I am your refuge and your strength, your shield and your deliverer. I have plans for you that will give you hope and a future" (*See Jeremiah 29:11*). "I will comfort you in your troubles, for I am the God of all comfort" *(See 2 Corinthians 1:3-4.)*

My dear friend, the Father sees your sorrow. Cast all your anxiety on him, because he cares for you (1 Peter 5:7). Cling to Him as you travel through the wilderness. Look for His expressions of love for you alone every day. The King of kings and Lord of lords will lead you safely through the abyss. He will bring hope into your heart as He leads you out of the darkness and into the sunshine.

There are times of laughter and rejoicing that are waiting for you, my beloved. For now, rest in Him, and know that your Father dearly loves you!

Heather

CHAPTER 6

—〜〜—

THE PRAYER ROOM

I am my beloved's and my beloved is mine.
—Song of Songs 6:3

Take me away with you—let us hurry!
Let the king bring me into his chambers.
—Song of Songs 1:4

Dearly Beloved:

I have a prayer room. It is a wonderful place where God and I spend time together, a sweet place of quiet rest and perfect peace. The feeling of God's presence is like spring rain falling gently on tulips and daffodils in the early morning hour. When I walk through the door, the problems and hurts of the day are left behind. God is in the little room, waiting for me.

I tell Him everything: all my hopes for the future, my frustrations of the present, and the disappointments of the past. And He patiently listens and puts His arms around me. He comforts me with His presence. God gives me strength to face another day. Sometimes He puts a word in my heart or brings a person to my mind to pray for. On other occasions, it is just a time for us alone. I like those moments best.

In the room, one small candle glows softly in the dark. Sometimes, when I stay longer than usual, the walls and ceiling radiate a heavenly light, and a sweet holiness permeates the room. I feel like I could touch Him then. And I am reluctant to leave His arms of love.

Every child needs a place where he can be alone with the Father. It doesn't have to be a room, but a special place set apart for you and God. Maybe it's just a favorite chair in a quiet corner or the space where you kneel beside your bed.

It's good to have personal time with the Lord. As you seek Him regularly, your moments with Him will become filled with rapturous delight. You will look forward to those times with great anticipation. And you will give the Father great pleasure.

In those quiet moments with Him, your Father will make you feel like you are the only person in the universe and that you are all who matters—just you alone. He loves you so much, my dear. You are His beloved. See what great love the Father has lavished on us, that we should be called children of God (1 John 3:1).

The Father will be anxiously waiting for you, my dear. He looks forward to those special times of communion even more than you do.

My friend let me invite you to spend time tonight with the Lord. He is eagerly waiting for you.

God loves you!
Heather

CHAPTER 7

—⚏—

THE HURRICANE

They are like a man building a house, who dug
down deep and laid the foundation on rock. When
a flood came, the torrent struck that house but
could not shake it, because it was well built.
—Luke 6:48

Dearly Beloved:

It was a windy day as I headed to work to my office in Richmond, Virginia several years ago. Warnings of a colossal hurricane were threatening the coast just one hundred miles away. People had started evacuating and headed toward safer ground. I was hoping it would go away, ignoring the warnings. Studiously, I worked on my daily tasks, trying to disregard the increasing wind as it began to pick up.

At 1:30 PM my manager came over to my desk and calmly told me to go home. The gusts of wind were increasing. I tried to still my fears as I went to the deck and got into my car, a small Toyota.

As I drove home, it felt like the wind was going to pick up the car and carry me along with it. My daughter had called earlier and invited me to her house to wait out the storm, but I decided to tough it out. I parked myself in front of the television and waited as the wind hollered and trees began to bend. Trying to forget the large oak tree inches from my bedroom window, I sat in my large recliner and focused on the nightly news.

At five-thirty that evening, my son came by. The lights were on, but it was only a matter of time before they would go out. He kindly offered to go to the store and buy me a lighter, just in case. Concerned, my son also tried to convince me to go home with him. But stubbornly, I said I could handle it, and he left to go home to his family.

Night came sooner than usual; the lights went off, and I was terrified. The winds became stronger, and rain poured. Because I was on the top floor, I decided to prepare for evacuation. I grabbed a bag, started packing some clothes, and put them in the hall. Looking around the small apartment, I took pictures off the wall and put them in the hall also, just in case the tree toppled over. I was ready to leave, although I had no idea where I was going. I knew I should have gone with my family, and panic rose up in me. The storm had grown stronger—around seventy miles per hour, my daughter told me over the phone. My little apartment was no match for it, and I wondered if I would survive.

I walked around, pacing, and suddenly, the Word of God came to mind. Even though I walk through the darkest valley, I will fear no evil, for you are with me (Psalm 23:4).

I remembered the words of Jesus: "Therefore everyone who hears these words of mine and puts them into practice is like a wise man who built his house on the rock. The rain came down, the streams rose, and the winds blew and beat against that house; yet it did not fall, because it had its foundation on the rock" (Matthew 7:24-25).

God was gently telling me that though there will be storms if I am grounded in Christ, He would always be with me and keep me safe. And indeed, as the hurricane hit in full force and the tree looked like it would definitely fall, I knew He would keep me safe, for I was His precious child!

You are too, my beloved. He will keep you in the eye of the storm, where it is quiet and calm, because He loves you passionately. When things are spiraling out of control all around you, the Father will protect you and comfort you with words of hope and love.

The storm subsided late that night. The tree did not fall, and I was safe. I called my daughter, and my kind son-in-law answered. Living on his farm, Lee knew all about storms. He assured me that all was well because of the sounds outside—tree frogs singing in the night. The songs affirmed, he said, that the storm was over, and everything would be all right.

I opened the window in my bedroom and lay on my bed, listening to the frogs on my tree. It was still standing, and I knew that God had kept me safe. He will keep you safe too, my beloved. Do not be afraid, for I am with you (Isaiah 43:5).

God loves you!

Heather

CHAPTER 8

—ɯ—

EXTRAVAGANT LOVE

"Because he loves me," says the
LORD, "I will rescue him;
I will protect him, for he acknowledges my name.
He will call on me, and I will answer him;
I will be with him in trouble,
I will deliver him and honor him.
With long life I will satisfy him and
show him my salvation."
—Psalm 91:14–16

Dearly Beloved:
Recently, I lost my job, and the pain has been excruciating. I feel lost and all alone. It's like going through a painful divorce. I wonder where God is; I feel like giving up. He gave me this job seven years ago, and now it is gone.

I don't know what to do, and my heart is heavy. I know that God loves me; I see signs of His extravagant love all around me.

Do you recognize His signs of love for you? Look closely. Ask Him to show you. He is always faithful. For me, it is cardinals. When I lost my husband and home, God showed up through the cardinals. Every time I feel discouraged, He sends cardinals to bless and comfort me. They remind me that God is with me and will always keep me safe in His arms.

Last night, as I looked out of the window, two large, bright red cardinals flew by me. I thought that was so unusual. Two males were flying together! This was unheard of—but not to our Father. He knew I desperately needed to see His love in an extraordinary way, so He sent two to remind me that He is always near.

I don't know where this journey will lead; I am afraid. But in His precious Word, God promises never to leave us nor forsake us *(See Hebrews 13:5).*

So look up, dearly beloved. The God of the universe is above the storm you are in *(See Psalm 29:10).* And even though everything is crashing around you, He is keeping you close to Him. Hold on, and you will feel His extravagant love just for you.

God loves you!
Heather

CHAPTER 9

—ᘰ—

LITTLE THINGS

How precious to me are your thoughts, God!
How vast is the sum of them!
Were I to count them,
they would outnumber the grains of sand—
when I awake, I am still with you.
—Psalm 139:17–18

Dearly Beloved:

Life is often hard. We struggle, toil, and hope that the future will be better for us and our loved ones. Often when we feel alone, our thoughts turn to God. We look for Him to act on our behalves in mighty ways. And many times He does, but God often demonstrates His love in small, seemingly insignificant ways that will bring life to our spirits and hope to our hearts.

The kindness of God leads to our repentance *(See Romans 2:4)*. He loves you, dearly beloved! He will show you how much in marvelous ways—sometimes big, but many times in small ways that will comfort you and let you know that He is near.

People experience God in special ways; for me, it's through the cardinals. They appear when I am going through a storm and need comforting. The lovely red birds remind me that God is holding me in His arms of love. They remind me not to be afraid of the valley of shadow of death, for He is with me. He tells me in His Word to be strong and courageous, for He goes before me and will lead me in the path of righteousness. I am His beloved child, His precious child, and nothing will keep Him from me—neither death nor life, neither angels nor demons, neither the present nor the future, nor any powers, neither height nor depth, nor anything else in all creation will be able to separate us from the love of God that is in Christ Jesus our Lord (Romans 8:38–39).

I see His love demonstrated through the love of brothers and sisters in Christ who come alongside me when I am struggling. I see His love demonstrated in a thousand ways by looking at His magnificent creation: deer leaping through the forest, a rushing waterfall, a breathtaking sunset, the power of the ocean waves, the drops of rain on spring flowers blooming in the early spring, the majesty of the stars shining brightly in the darkness, and the snow falling softly to the ground on a bitterly cold night.

Dear friend, you are passionately loved by Jesus Christ. As you journey through life, look everywhere for signs of His extravagant love for you.

God loves you!
Heather

CHAPTER 10

—⚇—

THE FATHER'S LOVE

For God so loved the world that he gave his
one and only Son, that whoever believes in
him shall not perish but have eternal life.
—John 3:16

The Spirit you received does not make you slaves,
so that you live in fear again; rather, the Spirit
you received brought about your adoption to
sonship. And by him we cry, "Abba, Father."
—Romans 8:15

Dearly Beloved:

We who have embraced Christ and surrendered our lives to Him have been adopted into the family of God. We will live forever with Him. What a glorious day that will be! All tears, suffering, and pain will be forever gone, and we will live forever with Jesus. We are His beloved sons and daughters.

Even though we make mistakes, He forgives us and showers us with mercy and grace to keep going.

This past week, I have been in the valley. Great loneliness settled around me, and pain consumed me. Sick and afraid, I was forced to lean completely on the Father. God is our provider. And my God will meet all your needs according to the riches of his glory in Christ Jesus (Philippians 4:19). Carefully, He led me through the darkness, one step at a time. With an aching head and a broken heart, I stumbled many times and almost gave up. But every time the thoughts came, I would get a surprise e-mail, phone message, or card saying, "Hang in there; God will get you through."

One particular night, after several days of suffering with a migraine, I was sitting in my recliner, trying to figure out what the problem was. All kinds of thoughts came into my head; perhaps I had developed TMJ or teeth grinding and not noticed. It had been years since I had suffered through that condition, and I blamed it on stress.

Head, neck, and ears pounding, I considered the ailment. I concentrated on the pain and thought hard about its origin. Abruptly, I noticed acute pain in my throat that I had not noticed before. Could this be the problem? I remembered a prescription for antibiotics from the prior year that I had not taken. I prayed, "God, if I still have them, please show me where they are." I slowly got out of the chair and went into the bathroom and carefully looked in the cramped linen closet. Underneath piles of stuff, I found a little bag from the pharmacy. Much to my surprise, there it was! I quickly took a dose and was amazed at what happened. Within one hour, the sore throat was gone, and my jaws relaxed. The headache subsided almost immediately!

God is true to His Word, dear friend. He will provide all of your needs. Look to Him as your protector, and you will not be disappointed. Keep your eyes on Christ. He cares for your every need, for you are His beloved child!

God loves you!
Heather

CHAPTER 11

—∞—

STORMS

The LORD himself goes before you and will be
with you; he will never leave you nor forsake you.
Do not be afraid; do not be discouraged.
—Deuteronomy 31:8

The LORD is good, a refuge in times of trouble.
He cares for those who trust in him.
—Nahum 1:7

You have been a refuge for the poor, a refuge
for the needy in their distress, a shelter from
the storm and a shade from the heat.
—Isaiah 25:4

Dearly Beloved:

The storms in our lives often strike without warning—the loss of a loved one, the loss of our home, the loss of hope. We may wonder if God is still with us or if He has abandoned us in our pain. His words are quite clear: "Be strong and courageous. Do not be afraid or terrified because of them, for the LORD your God goes with you; he will never leave you nor forsake you" (Deuteronomy 31:6).

Storms appear suddenly. They knock us off our feet; but we don't have to stay there. Paul said, "We are hard pressed on every side, but not crushed; perplexed, but not in despair; persecuted, but not abandoned; struck down, but not destroyed" (2 Corinthians 4:8-9).

Jesus sees your pain; He has experienced it Himself. He has walked in your shoes. He knows when you are discouraged, lonely, and brokenhearted. He is waiting to comfort you with His sweet words of love. Go to Him, my beloved. He is waiting for you.

God loves you!
Heather

CHAPTER 12

—ɷ—

A CUP OF COLD WATER

And if anyone gives even a cup of cold water to one
of these little ones who is my disciple, truly I tell you,
that person will certainly not lose their reward.
—Matthew 10:42

Dearly Beloved:

The verse above has always been meaningful to me. A simple act of kindness can be a powerful deed that brings a smile to a weary person and delights the Father.

Whenever someone shows up at my door, I immediately ask that person if he would like a glass of water. It doesn't matter who the person is; it could be a workman or someone who needs direction. Offering a drink of water demonstrates the love of Christ in a personal way. It quenches the thirst and lets the person know that someone cares. In a world that is often indifferent, this small act of kindness gives comfort and encouragement to a person who is struggling. It provides hope that someone cares and helps that individual continue on his way.

Dearly beloved, don't overlook the significance of a cup of cold water. You are serving others and glorifying Christ.

God loves you!
Heather

CHAPTER 13

—ɱ—

MY PROVIDER

And my God will meet all your needs according
to the riches of his glory in Christ Jesus.
—Philippians 4:19

Dearly Beloved:

Twenty years ago this week, my marriage ended. I reflected on that yesterday, and my thoughts naturally turned to God and how He had faithfully provided for me, a single lady, for all those years. Looking back, I can see Him gently encouraging me to get up out of the bed and quietly reassuring me to go to school and then to work. I was working on my undergraduate degree at the time.

I could not have made it without the Father challenging me to take one step at a time and leave the worry of the future to Him. Many days, I didn't want to get out of bed, but I knew the Father was with me as He comforted and strengthened me to face another day. I stayed close to Him. I had to. Without Him,

I knew I would not make it. My energy was depleted, and my mind and emotions were broken and sad. I had a hard time eating and sleeping, and I lost a great deal of weight. Still, the Lord would not let me quit!

When I told Him I did not want to read the books that were required for the fall literature class, a beautiful young woman suddenly came through the door of the ladies' restroom. She was holding a cane and stood behind me. God spoke quietly into my heart, "She would love to read those books!" I immediately repented of my bad attitude. Slowly and unwillingly, I went to classes and work. I held tightly to His hand, as I had no idea what the future would bring.

And now, twenty years later, I pause and reflect on how my Father provided for me for so long: He moved me seven times to safe, quiet places to teach me more of Him. He gave me the strength and perseverance to earn my Bachelor of Science degree in psychology and my master's degree in social work. He spoke stories of His faithfulness into my heart that resulted in a dear little book named *Dearest Samantha: I Love You!!!!* that was published in 2012.

God tests my patience, endurance, acts of kindness, and ability to forgive and be forgiven. Most importantly, He taught me how to love not only people I know, but also those whom I don't. He gives me the fervor to pray for every person I see as I am driving down the road.

He provided me with job opportunities that I wasn't even looking for. One evening, I was complaining to the Father about something insignificant. He spoke softly to my heart. "Haven't I always provided for you?" He asked.

I was immediately ashamed and said, "Yes, You have. I am sorry, Father. You have always provided for me."

The twenty years of learning more about Jesus have not been in vain. God has done a miracle in my life.

He has given me a passionate love for Christ. He has given me a deep love for humanity. He has given me a hunger for His Word. He has given me compassion for the lost. He has filled my heart with incredible joy. And even though times may be hard, I know my Daddy loves me and will continue to take care of me!

Dearly beloved, you are the apple of His eye *(See Psalm 17:8)*. You are beautiful and deeply cherished by the Father. So rest in Him, sweet friend, and know that the Father will provide for *all* of your needs, for He has promised this in His Word.

As you spend time with Him, your faith will rise as you watch Him working perfectly in your life to satisfy the longings of your heart and to bring Him great glory.

God loves you!
Heather

CHAPTER 14

—ɯɯ—

DREAMS

The LORD will vindicate me;
your love, LORD, endures forever—
do not abandon the works of your hands.
—Psalm 138:8

"For I know the plans I have for you," declares
the LORD...plans to prosper you and not to harm
you, plans to give you hope and a future."
—Jeremiah 29:11

Dearly Beloved:

The highest honor on this side of heaven is to worship God and give Him glory, power, and praise, for He alone is worthy!

To make sense of life, it is important to establish goals at an early age. Children love to play the game "What do you want to be when you grow up?" Often, they may still be asking the same question years later if they haven't discovered their destinies, the reason they were created. But God in His great love already knew what the child was created to be before he had even been born. All the days ordained for me were written in your book before one of them came to be (Psalm 139:16). He gives each child unique gifts chosen for a specific purpose in life. Even the timing of a child's existence is critical to the Father's role for him!

Each of us has extraordinary gifts and talents that the Father, if we let Him, can use to do great things for His glory! Consider the fishermen who fished all night in vain. Early in the morning, Jesus stood on the shore and said to the disciples, "Throw your net on the right side of the boat and you will find some." When they did, they were unable to haul the net in because of the large number of fish (John 21:4-6).

God made you uniquely different from anyone else in the universe. He made you special and gifted you with extraordinary talents. His perfect plan will give you deep purpose and meaning. If you do not know His purpose for your life, ask the Father to show you.

He will bring much joy into your heart as He speaks softly of His great plans for you—plans that will bring you delight and advance His kingdom on earth.

God loves you!
Heather

CHAPTER 15

—w—

THE KEY

Jesus answered, "I am the way and the truth and the life. No one comes to the Father except through me."
—John 14:6

Dearly Beloved:

One late summer evening, I arrived home and was surprised to see my grass man still there. His car was filled with sticks and leaves from my yard; there was hardly enough room for him. He appeared anxious and was afraid that I would be angry because he had not left yet. I asked Bruce what was wrong. He told me that he had lost his car key and couldn't find it. I live on a third of an acre, and it was getting dark. How would we ever find it?

I ran into the house and got a flashlight; it was little, however, and not effective. For some odd reason, I turned on the front yard light but forgot to turn on the back house light. Bruce said the key evidently fell out of his pocket; there was no telling where it was!

God sees your struggles, precious friend. When you don't know what to do, ask the Father to show you. He is always faithful!

While Bruce was combing the back yard in the dark using only the little flashlight, I went into the house and prayed fervently, "Father, You know where the key is. Please show it to us." A simple prayer – yes – but our God is all-powerful, and He answered!

Five minutes later, Bruce showed up at the door. "I found it!" he exclaimed. It was lying under the old oak tree in the backyard. I was blown away! The Father not only heard, but He also quickly led Bruce to the right spot. Isn't God wonderful?

Jesus is our key to eternal life. There is no other way to heaven. He gave His life so that we might have everlasting life. So thank Him today, dearly beloved, for dying for your sins, for giving His broken body and precious blood so that you will be forever with Him in eternity!

God loves you!
Heather

CHAPTER 16

—ɯ—

FORGIVENESS

Love your enemies and pray for those who persecute
you, that you may be children of your Father in heaven.
—Matthew 5:44-45

Dearly Beloved:

Forgiveness is often difficult to do. When we are angry or disappointed over life situations, we frequently want revenge. We want to blame someone for the hurt he has caused and the pain that is unbearable.

If we choose to hang on to unforgiveness, the deadly poison starts to eat away our minds, bodies, and spirits. We become bitter and disgruntled with life. Often, unforgiveness affects our loved ones; they distance themselves from the person we have unwittingly become. And the individual we blame may not even know or care. That person is enjoying his life and may not give us a second thought.

But if we choose to let go of the unforgiveness and give it to God, we will feel immediate relief. We are the ones who are set free; we are the ones who will soar like eagles, for the load will be taken off our backs as we give the burden to our Father.

Many years ago, I was at that point and didn't even know it. My marriage had ended, but I was still living in the past. It was somehow easier than facing the future. But the Father knew I was only deceiving myself.

One Sunday, I attended both morning services. We were having Holy Communion, and it was my responsibility to prepare the elements. The message was on *Unforgiveness*. The pastor didn't mince words. He said, "If you need to forgive someone, stand up." All around the congregation, people stood up and surrendered their unforgiveness to God. I knew that there was a reason I was attending both services. Two messages required me to choose forgiveness for two different people and stand up!

I felt like a bird that had just learned to fly. Gone were the hurt and anger, and joy filled my spirit. I was free!

Not long ago, God brought to mind a person whom I needed to ask forgiveness. It had been decades, but God had not forgotten. So one morning I drove to her home, got out of the car, and walked up the steps to her front door.

I rang the doorbell and waited. Soon, I heard the footsteps of someone, and the door slowly opened. My friend of the past was standing there before me. I hadn't seen her in twenty years. She looked pleased to see me and invited me in.

We chatted awhile, talked about our children and grandchildren, and discussed the struggles we both had faced.

Toward the end of the visit, I shared the true reason I was there. It was to ask her forgiveness.

When our children were quite small, both of our families attended a little Methodist church not far away. It was one Saturday morning when she came. I was painting my son's room a wild green, and she came in to talk to me. "Heather," she said, "will you walk down the aisle with me and rededicate our lives together to Christ?"

"No," I said without hesitation. I didn't want to and never gave it a second thought. I had put Jesus on the back burner for years and was not ready or willing to make such a life-changing commitment.

She never showed her disappointment, and I forgot about it until the Father reminded me. At my visit, I reminded her of how I had responded to her invitation to rededicate our lives to Christ. I asked her forgiveness and went over and hugged her.

She didn't say anything, but she smiled, and I think she knew I was genuinely sorry. Our visit continued for a few minutes more, and I promised to keep in touch. As I left, I asked the Father to bless my friend; my heart felt lighter as I headed home.

Is there someone you need to forgive, dear friend? Or is there someone you need to ask for forgiveness? Please ask the Lord to help you take this courageous action, and reconcile the relationship. You will be blessed mightily and bring the Father much joy.

God loves you!
Heather

CHAPTER 17

—〰—

HOME

Take delight in the LORD, and he will
give you the desires of your heart.
—Psalm 37:4

Dearly Beloved:
Two years ago, I was lying in my bed, sick with the flu and in excruciating pain with shingles. I had been ill for days and was miserable. "I cannot die on this pike," I cried to the Father. I lived three houses from a large turnpike with cars, trucks, and fire engines rushing by.

The house was cute. My parents helped me buy it, and we worked hard on making it a home. However, ever since I had lost my first home where my husband and I had raised our children, I longed to go back there. It was close to the woods, and there were several acres between us and our neighbors. My home comforted me, but I had been gone for eighteen years after my marriage ended.

I was getting older and had moved several times since then. I had asked God to take me back home many times, but it always seemed He was saying, "Not yet."

One Sunday morning several years earlier, while living in an apartment, I was leaving my bedroom, heading for church. At that moment, I turned around, and there was a quiet hush in the room. A soft glow penetrated the darkness. I felt like I was in the presence of God. "You are going home, Heather," He spoke tenderly to my heart.

"When?" I asked.

"In My time," He replied.

What a tremendous comfort that was! God had promised that I would go home. My spirit soared as I drove to church. I didn't know it then, but it was actually several years before the miracle took place, while I was sick in bed in the little house on the pike.

Many people prayed for me while I was ill. My church came alongside me and called and sent letters of encouragement. My thoughtful manager allowed me the time required to get well.

Several weeks later, fully recovered, I happened to look on the Internet for my desired location in Mechanicsville, Virginia. The road was close to my former home. Much to my surprise, there was a house for sale! It looked almost identical to the house where I had lived for thirty years. It was back in the woods, about a mile away. I was blown over! Pictures of the rooms resembled the house I had left.

I excitedly called the real estate agent and asked when I could see it. We made an appointment for the next day, and my daughter met me there.

Custom-made shutters adorned each window; hardwood floors flowed through the entire house. There were three bedrooms, two baths, a large living room, and a den with a fireplace. In front of the house was an acre of beautiful woods. Behind the house was a large converted garage with heat and air and a walk-in attic—more than enough room for my thirty years of stuff! And behind that were forty more acres of woods.

The house had been on the market for five months; one hundred people had visited it, and *no one* had made an offer. The seller had reduced the house by approximately $15,000, which put the price within my budget!

God had not forgotten me. He was making a way while I was home sick. Four months later, I moved into the perfect home for me! He will do the same for you, dearly beloved. You are His precious child. Be still before the LORD and wait patiently for him (Psalm 37:7). Take delight in the LORD, and he will give you the desires of your heart (Psalm 37:4).

God loves you!
Heather

CHAPTER 18

—ɯ—

MY DADDY

See what great love the Father has lavished
on us, that we should be called children
of God! And that is what we are!
—1 John 3:1

Dearly Beloved:

I love talking about God. He is everything to me: my Savior, my Provider, my Protector, my Healer, my Comforter, and my Father. When I am with friends and family who love Jesus, we always talk about how wonderful God is. He has always kept me safe, even when I walked my own way and did not really understand how much He cared for me.

Once when I was nine years old, I wandered into a secluded park by myself. No one knew where I was. I stayed for a while— too long to be alone. I could have easily have gotten hurt. But the Father had His eye on me and kept me safe.

One evening, I had dinner with a good friend of mine. We both went to the same church, and our conversation naturally turned to Jesus and stories of His faithfulness. We stayed for a couple of hours, but it only seemed like a few minutes. I loved sharing and hated to see the evening draw to a close.

I drove away thinking about our lovely time together. On my way home, I stopped at the grocery store to buy a few items. As I was sitting in my car, God spoke to my heart. He said, "Do you know why you love Me so much?"

"I have no clue," I responded.

The Father said, "I am the Daddy you never had."

Tears of joy came to my eyes, and the realization of the truth flooded my heart. My own father had left when I was just five. I rarely saw him and never spent holidays with him—not even my birthday. At the age of eleven, he disappeared for good, and I never saw him again.

When I was eleven, my mother married a quiet, gentle man who loved me. He was kind to me and provided for our family. Back in the fifties, however, men didn't often show their feelings. He never held me in his lap or kissed me. It just wasn't done. I didn't feel special, and there was something missing deep inside of me.

It wasn't until my son grew up and had children of his own that I realized what I had been missing as a child. I watched as he sang to his young daughter and held his little son, dancing to a special tune. Once when my granddaughter was only two, she became upset because her brother got some much-needed shirts that were on sale. She didn't get any and started crying. Her mother and I watched the little girl march upstairs, go into her room, grab her blanket, and come down and climb into her daddy's lap where she was comforted.

I suddenly saw, for the first time, how important it is to have a daddy who loves you and is always there to comfort and reassure you. That is our Father. He is our Daddy, and He loves us unconditionally. No matter what you do, His love will never change; He is always there to hold you in His arms of love.

If you don't know Him as your Daddy, ask Him to reveal Himself to you. You will not be disappointed, for the Father is the best Daddy you will ever have! And you will know how precious you are to Him—how much He treasures you.

God bless you, dear friend. Know that your Father dearly loves you!

Heather

CHAPTER 19

—∞—

GLORY

And we all, who with unveiled faces contemplate
the Lord's glory, are being transformed into
his image with ever-increasing glory, which
comes from the Lord, who is the Spirit.
—2 Corinthians 3:18

I consider that our present sufferings are not worth
comparing with the glory that will be revealed in us.
—Romans 8:18

Dearly Beloved:

One winter evening, while lying in my bed ill, I felt miserable and alone. The room was quiet, and darkness made its way down the silent street. I lay there, thinking about what was next in my life. The first few months of the year had been difficult; I was getting older and couldn't begin to think of the future.

Suddenly, without warning, the entire atmosphere of the room changed. It was like I left the room and went into another. A quite hush permeated the area; I felt like I was on holy ground. I could almost sense angels in the little bedroom. I didn't make a sound: I just lay there and absorbed the breathtaking moment.

The house seemed so far away as I was transported to another place filled with the presence of God. Peace enveloped me, and a quiet joy permeated by heart. Gone were illness, pain, depression, and hopelessness. I was caught up in the glory of God.

Have you experienced Him, dearly beloved? He longs to take you away with Him into a world you cannot imagine—a world where Jesus lives to enjoy Him forever. One day we will be forever with our Savior in that glorious place! Know that even now Jesus is preparing a place for you *(See John 14:2)*.

... Our citizenship is in heaven. And we eagerly await a Savior from there, the Lord Jesus Christ, who, by the power that enables him to bring everything under his control, will transform our lowly bodies so they will be like his glorious body (Philippians 3:20-21).

Dearly beloved, Jesus is waiting with great excitement for the day He will take you home to be forever with Him!

God loves you!
Heather

CHAPTER 20

—ɯ—

COMFORT

Praise be to the God and Father of our Lord Jesus
Christ, the Father of compassion and the God of
all comfort, who comforts us in all our troubles, so
that we can comfort those in any trouble with the
comfort we ourselves receive from God. For just
as we share abundantly in the sufferings of Christ,
so also our comfort abounds through Christ.
—2 Corinthians 1:3-5

Dearly Beloved:
You are cherished by God. He loves you so much.
He is your Father. You are His child. He is always with you,
loving you and watching over you. He will make a way. He will
protect you. If you are frightened and alone, look to your Daddy.
If you feel hopeless, look to your Father.

Dearly beloved, your Father is Creator of the universe and
has a magnificent plan to enrich your life. You, in turn, will be
equipped to offer hope and encouragement to others around

you and beyond. My friend, He will strengthen you and bring joy to your soul. He will make a way.

The Father will reveal Himself to you in a glorious way. And when that day comes, look up and rejoice for your King is on His throne and you belong forever to Him!

God loves you!
Heather